MW01629987

The CASTLE in the SWAMP

The CASTLE in the SWAMP

The story of Solomon's Castle

Peggy Reilly Solomon

Little Silver Books

ISBN: 0-9712556-1-X

Little Silver Books
4533 Solomon Road
Ona, FL 33865
www.solomonscastle.com

This book is for all our visitors who over the years have enjoyed Howard's wonderful art and unique sense of humor, for all those who want to know how it all began, from the early years.

*

And so:

"Once upon a time..........."

PROLOGUE

Howard Solomon was born in Rochester, New York, in 1935. He began wood carving at age four and metal working as a teenager. After leaving school and fulfilling his military obligation, he moved to St Petersburg, Florida where he found employment in the construction and boat building trades. By the 60's he had moved into metal and wood sculpture, which he sold through his own galleries in the Bahamas and Miami.
His work has been noted by all the media, including the Associated Press, Boston Globe, Wall Street Journal, and New York Times and has been featured on many television productions in the United States and Europe.

*

Howard Solomon came to Hardee County, Florida in January of 1972. Finding swampland affordable, he was able to purchase 40 acres where Horse Creek meandered through marshy land for a mile and had a white sandy beach.

He set up quarters in a mobile home on his land while deciding what type of permanent home to build. He would need a large structure to house his workshop, stained glass studio and to store his many wood and metal sculptures. As the rainy season began and he realized he needed to build something high off the ground. A man's home is his castle? Then a castle it would be! (Palaces were just too expensive to furnish.)

Fill would be needed to raise the ground under the castle, so Howard began by digging a moat. The main structure was the workshop. One side was a three story tower and a two story tower on the other side. Bedrooms were in the top two stories of the first, while the second housed a room for metal and wood sculptures, with his study and library above.

Now we are getting turrets!

Sept. 7, 1972 The Herald-Advocate Page 5-

Hardee County's Answer To Buckingham Palace

This aerial view shows the castle built by Hardee County sculptor Howard Solomon along the banks of Horse Creek in the Lily area. Solomon is building the structure mostly by himself. The widower lives there with his children. He sculpts with such materials as wood and metal and is a world recognized artist. A fellow artist, Jim McGee, lives there part-time, and Solomon hopes to attract other artists to his Horse Creek estate. He and McGee came here from the Bahamas. Solomon conducts open house to the public at his place the last Sunday of each month.

Curiosity overcame the citizens of Hardee County, and Howard was asked to speak at the Kiwanis Club, and encouraged to open 'Solomon's Castle' to the public. This he did, although it would only be for one day, on the last Sunday of each month.

News-Press/Jeffrey Core

Sculptor Howard Solomon surrounds himself with his creations

The castle as it appeared in 1972, when first opened to the public

Howard Solomon and his metal sculpture,
'Confusion'.

The next stage was the actual living quarters, Howard Solomon's 'HOME'. Construction began in 1978.

All of the work was done by Howard, himself, except the main concrete pour and setting the trusses. It would take him two full years until by early 1981, he was ready to move in.

The kitchen has an elevator that goes to the bedroom above.

The living room looks out to a very spacious back porch.

Hardee Sculptor And His Castle Featured On Television Monday Night

One day, while reading the local newspaper, Howard saw an advertisement for used printing plates-- 'good for patching a roof or a chicken coop-- and suddenly had a vision of a shiny castle!

One of the first postcards

Solomon's Castle became very popular on the last Sunday of the month. People started coming from other states and television stations began doing specials on this unique creation built by one man. The castle began opening every day except Monday, in 1984. Solomon's Castle became a 'must see' adventure for winter visitors. Solomon's Castle also became a unique addition for tour bus operators, antique car clubs and motorcycle groups.

A view from the far side of the moat showing the castle with the living quarters completed before the porch and carport were added.

Another new project began in 1984. The construction of the East Wing was built as a guest room. It is called the 'Blue Moon Room', and is for friends who want to spend the night in a castle and see 'what goes on here after dark'.

To allow for more gallery space in the castle, Howard built a new workshop, a short walk from the castle.

Gates now welcome visitors to the castle grounds.

Howard stamped out a yellow brick road using leftover paint from other projects and a sponge mop.

Now he was in a dilemma. The East Wing was finished, the new workshop was finished, and galleries were finished. He needed a new project. While going through his storage barns, he discovered a large bell. A bell needs a bell tower and thus began the next project. The bell tower has 10 nursery rhyme windows and three large bells. As the bell tower was being built, the old metal siding was removed and replaced with the printing plates. Now the entire castle sparkled in the sun.

The building of the bell tower turned into a family project. The nursery rhyme window patterns were designed by his sister, Billie.

Solomon's Castle had a moat. What better place to put a boat? The next project was to build a 65 foot replica of a Spanish galleon. He started the boat by submerging three telephone poles 10 feet deep into the moat floor.

He then added more pilings, 105, to be exact, and then started adding the flooring.

The ship's masts were made from cypress. An American flag and Jolly Roger were raised, and the hull was closed in.

The stern, which faces the swamp, has a rudder and port holes. The sides went up and were painted. The cannon, made from irrigation pipe, went into the gun ports. So far they have never been fired......

Sails were put in place. Then came the Crow's Nest and a ship's bell. Howard built a seven foot diameter ship's wheel.

One of the big stained glass windows in the stern of the ship is a pirate charting his course. The window was designed by Howard's friend, Guy LaBree, and took Howard over two weeks to complete.

The boat became 'The Boat in the Moat ' restaurant and is run by Howard's daughter, Alane and her husband, Dean. The restaurant serves all homemade food and caters to parties, weddings and luaus. You name it, Alane and Dean can do it!

There is seating inside or outside on the patio, and during the season, a musician plays on the patio.

The great wall went up surrounding the castle grounds.

From the leftover parts and pieces of the concrete wall, Howard built the concrete horse.

The next project was a lighthouse for the 'Boat in the Moat' restaurant. Construction began in March of 2003.

First, all the support beams were put in place.
Then the flooring was added.

The roof structure was added.

The metal was added and the top was now ready for the beacon, (to save all ships in Horse Creek). Then Howard gave the Lily Lighthouse its unique pattern.... it was time for the windows.

All the windows in the tower of the lighthouse represent lighthouses from around the country.

Hatters, Absecon,
Canaveral,
Cape Lookout,
Hilton Head,
even our own 'Lily lighthouse'

Time for a new project. Howard went to Texas on vacation. He just happened to see the Alamo and thought that a replica of the Alamo would make a wonderful addition to his accomplishments. So in September of 2007, he cleared the ground for the 'Alashmo', (he doesn't plagiarize). This was to be built next to the workshop.

First a slab was poured.

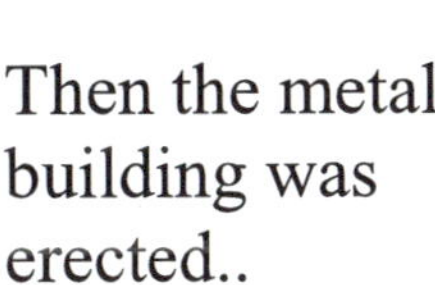

Then the metal building was erected..

The inside was finished.

And now comes the fun part, the Alamo facade!

Cover the frame work with plywood.

Frame out the windows.

Cover the plywood with tar paper.

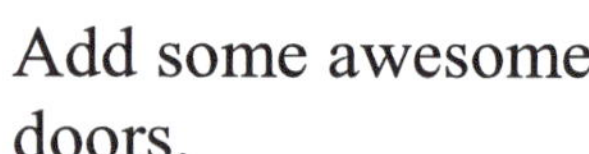

Add some awesome doors.

Stucco is applied and worked into a design of adobe brick.

Then he added the porch roof and the columns.

The' Alashmo' is guarded by a replica of a Civil War cannon also built by Howard.

The 'Alashmo' features a throne room and throne.

Through out the years, with all the large construction going on, Howard still kept up with his art work. There were many large oil drum sculptures, wood montages and keeping the gift shop shelves filled with his whimsical smaller pieces.

Many uses for oil drums

Wood sculpture

Universal joints

Brake shoes

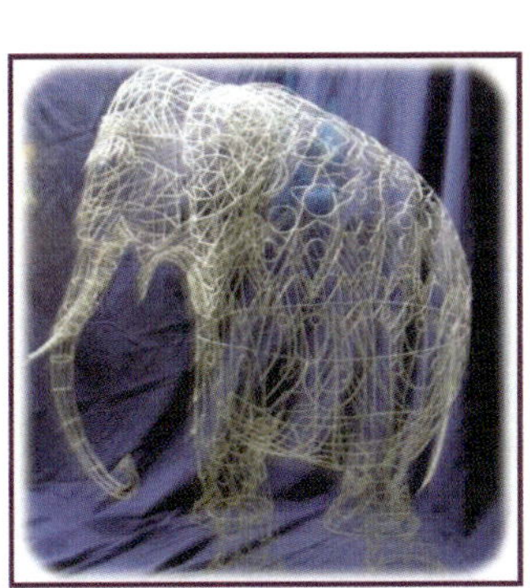

Wire coat hangers, chess table and chairs

Howard also created many commission pieces we call 'Art in Other Places'.

The stainless steel horse can be seen outside the Historical Building in Cortez, Florida.

A replica of 'The Frog Prince', privately owned and resides on Siesta Key

A stained glass door for a private home.

At the 'Ripley's Believe It or Not', in Gatlinburg, TN, you can see a full size horse made from coat hangers.

While recuperating from heart surgery in 2003, Howard received a get well card from a friend. It was a picture of a painting by Matisse. So began 'The Masters à la Solomon'. Among them are:

The 'Masters' series has been done as wood montage or steel.

Picasso's 'Jacqueline with Flowers'

The inspiration was Matisse's 'Still Life with Grendes'.

Picasso's 'Woman with Tambourine

Kandinsky's 'Upwards'

He also has Modigliani and Toulouse-Lautrec

He also created many of his own wood montages.
Some of them are:

Gotta have a 'Red Hat Lady'

'Howard by Howard'

'Picture Yourself on a Sailboat'

Howard's WMD is a 'Weapon of MOUSE destruction'

'Jake LaMotta', the Raging Bull

Howard's latest passion is collecting antique cars He specializes in cars older than he is. He now has acquired 13 of these classic cars.

Solomon's Castle contains over 500 works of his art. It is family owned and operated. The tour through the castle is guided, (Howard's art needs explaining!). It is a humorous tour colored by Howard's unique sense of humor, which is 'tongue-in-cheek' and full of puns. The tour includes the art galleries and the lower floor of the Solomon family living quarters, ending at the 'Boat in the Moat' restaurant, where there is seating for 250 people. During the winter season, there is a musician on the outside patio. The restaurant is also open on Friday and Saturday nights for late dining.

The castle's gift shop has numerous pieces of Howard's quirky art.

And so our story ends for now, but without a final chapter. We now have 90 acres, boundless imagination and there are so many more puns. What will happen next...........?

An Extraordinary Person
Sidney Karlin May 1988

Howard S. Solomon
distinctively unique
built himself a castle
that overlooks Horse Creek

Sculptor, welder, window stainer
man of accomplishments skill
his monument priceless container
created to express his will

All sorts of scraps bits and pieces
were used for fabrication
of ideas which came to mind
from his imagination

Hyperactive of genius quality
practically from birth
he kept his parents busy
with never any dearth

Of excitement wonderment
of that which was to come
from an incredible fertile mind
which could never be humdrum

At age four suddenly
he reveled his future bent
a razor blade a piece of wood
on which he carved and spent

Hours in a corner
steeped in concentration
finally he stepped forth
to show his first creation

Amazing unbelievable
how a tender lad
could conceive of what he did
but voila he surely had

A truck drawn by a car
with wheels that had full motion
astounding both the thought and not
to carry out this notion

This was the start of a career
now world renowned
countless works of his
can readily be found

In museums private collections
wherever art is shown
his name is recognizable
an artist well known

Emotions overwhelm one
as transient visitor
the artifacts seem endless
wall to wall and door to door

The patter of his docent
(who is his precious wife)
amusing and descriptive
brings everything to life

You come away awestruck
thrilled with sights this seems
fantastic mind-boggling
almost like a dream

Witness to compositions
original and rare
perceptive remarkable
a privilege to see and share

Huzzahs hurrahs to such as he
who deserves a special niche
and through his master craftsmanship
makes others feel so rich.

About the Author

Peggy has been at the castle building site for 25 years, observing, helping, climbing scaffolding and producing the Prince, 'heir to the throne'. Her green thumb is responsible for the landscaping that enhances the castle grounds. Queen Peggy gives castle tours and manages the other docents. Her 25 years as a nurse in her life before the castle, has greatly extended the productivity and life of Howard. Peggy is truly the Queen of the Castle, with a capitol ‘Q’.

Made in the USA
Charleston, SC
04 February 2010